Abuse is Not My Story

Coloring Companion

The Abuse is Not My Story Coloring Companion contains illustrations from the book Abuse is Not My Story. Images are light and designed to encourage Survivors on their journey to heal from abuse.

Victoria Elise Michael

ISBN 978-0-9983601-1-9

Cover design MD Bulbul Ahmed and Samantha Gustafson

Illustrations by Samantha Gustafson

Coloring designs by Dipak Kushwah

Book layout design by Svetlana Kotova

For Worldwide Distribution, Printed in the United States of America.

To protect the privacy of some of the individuals referred to, names, places, and other details have been changed.

Author's Note: This publication is designed to share a personal journey to freedom from abuse. It is sold with the understanding that the author is not engaged in rendering psychological, financial, legal, or other professional services. If expert assistance or counseling is needed, the services of a competent professional should be sought.

www.AbuseisNOTmystory.com

Abuse is NOT my Story

My Story is Created by the

Decisions I Make.

I Did NOT make the

Decision to be Abused.

I am thankful for these friends who
have been part of my life...

I am thankful for these mentors who have been part of my life...

My goals for counseling are...

I am beautiful.

DREAMS

I believe I can do great things.

I dream about...

Boundaries I have set because I care about myself include...

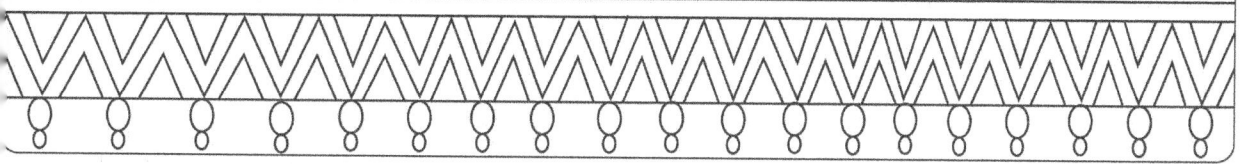

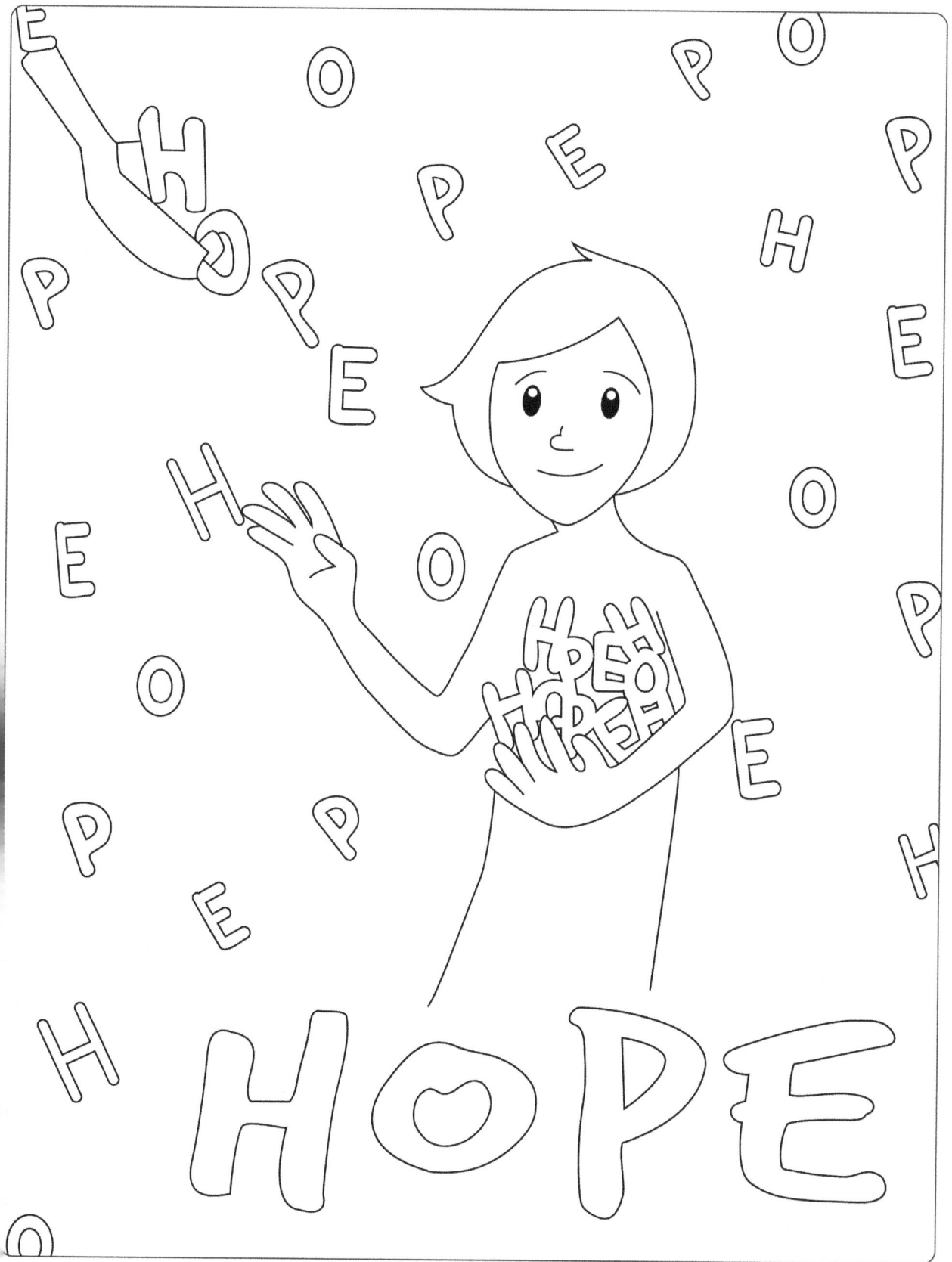

I am loved
with an
everlasting
love.

Jeremiah 31:3
NIV

You are my hiding place;
You will protect me from trouble
and surround me with songs of deliverance.

Psalm 32:7
NIV

He knows me!

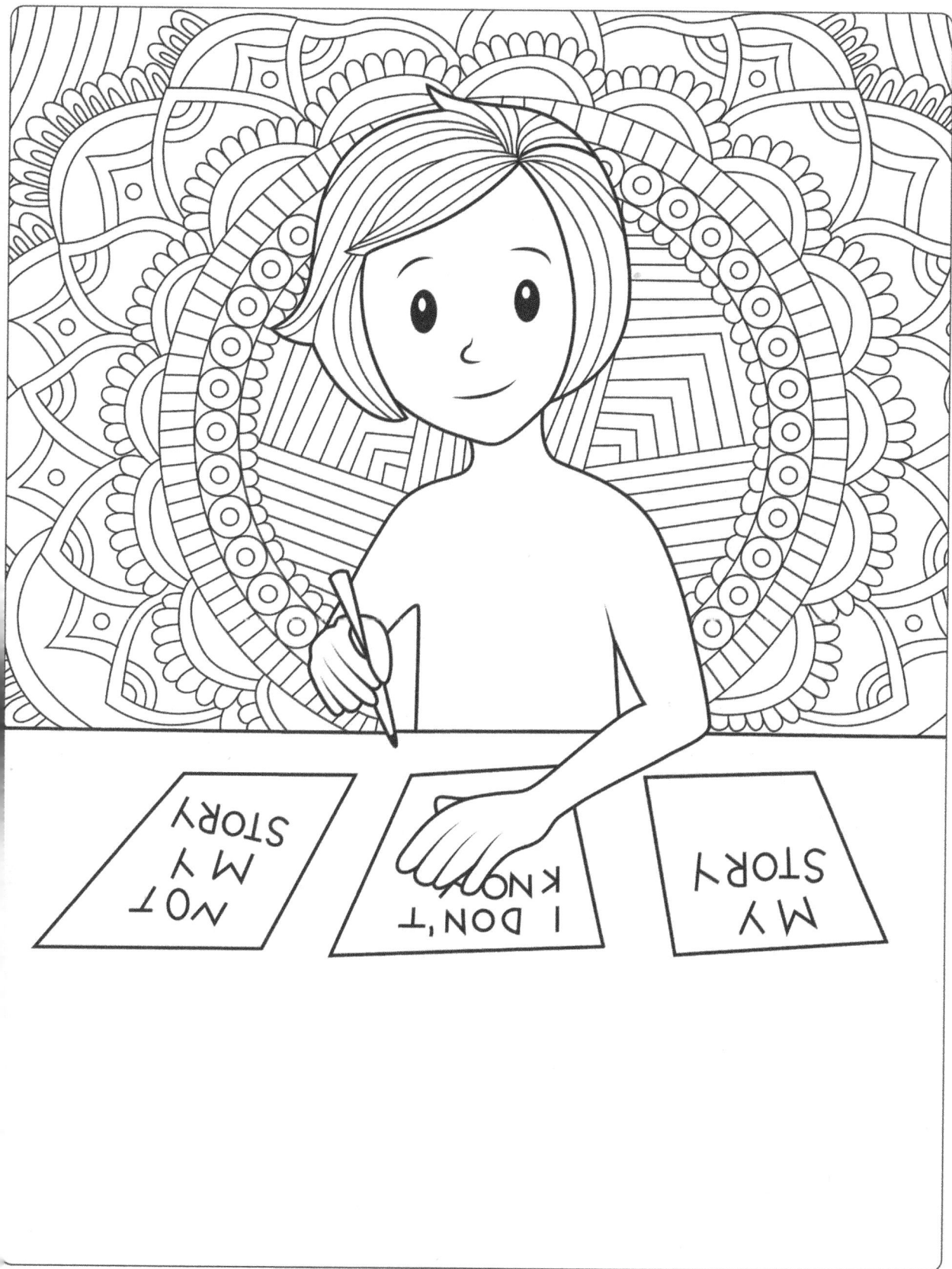

My Story

Not My Story

I Don't Know

I am unique,
special, important, and loved by God!

www.ingramcontent.com/pod-product-compliance
Lightning Source LLC
Chambersburg PA
CBHW080552030426
42337CB00024B/4853